A SHEPHERD'S JOURNEY

A PARABLE FOR ALL AGES

Written by Joanne Scholl

WestBow Press books may be ordered through booksellers or by contacting:

WestBow Press
A Division of Thomas Nelson & Zondervan
1663 Liberty Drive
Bloomington, IN 47403
www.westbowpress.com
844-714-3454

All Scriptures are taken from the Holy Bible, NEW INTERNATIONAL VERSION®, NIV® Copyright © 1973, 1978, 1984, 2011 by Biblica, Inc.® Used by permission. All rights reserved worldwide.

ISBN: 979-8-3850-0795-0 (sc)
ISBN: 979-8-3850-0801-8 (e)

Library of Congress Control Number: 2023917646

Print information available on the last page.

WestBow Press rev. date: 10/5/2023

Hi! My name is Willie. I guess I'm known as a hired hand out in this neck of the woods. I live just down the hill from a beautiful field that has become home to a big flock of sheep.

As I work my yard every day, I often watch – sometimes even stare, at the shepherd in charge of those sheep. He works so hard.

I wonder if that's why he asked me if I was looking for more work.

Yup! There he is again. Can you believe that shepherd thought I might need more work? I can see why he needs help, but was he actually thinking of me?

I see what it would take to work with him. I can't imagine caring for a bunch of smelly sheep! No Way!

"The man runs away because he is a hired hand and cares nothing for the sheep."
John 10:13

I can't believe the dedication of this shepherd.
He walks for miles just to find them good green
pastures to graze in.

"He makes me lie down in green pastures"
Psalm 23:2

He even searches for small still creeks, so the sheep will drink. I've heard they won't drink from rushing water because the noise will scare them away. He sure seems to care a lot about them.

"He leads me beside still waters"
Psalm 23:2

Look at him now! It looks like he's talking to those sheep like they were his family or something! He says he can even tell them apart. I sure don't know how! They all look alike to me!

"I know my sheep, and my sheep know me"
John 10:14

There goes that one sheep wandering off again. That shepherd always goes to find him, no matter what it takes, he never gives up!

"If a man has a hundred sheep and one of them of them gets lost, what will he do? Won't he leave the ninety-one others and go to search for the one that is lost until he finds it?"
Luke 15:14

Oh no! Look out!

One of his sheep runs for the same huge thorn bush every time, they don't seem very smart. Why does that shepherd care so much?

8

Wow, look how cut and torn the shepherd is, but the sheep looks like he doesn't have a scratch! That shepherd sure has shed a lot of blood, all for the mistakes of those silly sheep!

"The good shepherd sacrifices his life for the sheep"
John 10:11

I heard about one really stubborn sheep. He named him Jo. That stubborn sheep always ran his own way. Boy! Was he fast! He would run towards that highway in a split second.

"Even though I walk through the valley of the shadow of death, I fear no evil"
Psalm 23:4

"We all wander away like lost sheep"
Psalm 119:176

That shepherd has run after and saved that stubborn thing more times than I can count. He usually risk his own life doing it. I wouldn't risk my life to save a stubborn sheep!

"I lay down my life for the sheep"
John 10:15

One day I saw him carrying that sheep named Jo. I figured a truck must have finally hit him. He was walking calmly up the hill with Jo draped around his shoulders.

"And when he has found the lost sheep,
He will joyfully carry it home on his shoulders."
John 15:5

12

I couldn't believe what the shepherd said when I asked about it! He actually watched as little Jo went on yet another highway run. He saw him heading for the same really rough and rocky terrain. Sure enough, the sheep tripped and fell, breaking his leg, right before he got to that busy highway.

The shepherd carefully wrapped little Jo and placed him on his shoulders, knowing that he would have to carry him everywhere until he healed. That's a lot of care and carrying for one little sheep!

"We all like sheep, have strayed away."
Isaiah 53:6.

"He will carry the lambs on his arms,
holding them close to his heart."
Isaiah 40:11

But you know, little Jo never left his shepherd's side again. It's like he finally understood how much he needed the shepherd's guidance and protection.

"He restores my soul. He guides me in paths of righteousness for His name sake."
Psalm 23:3

I can't imagine what job that shepherd might possibly want me to do.

I have noticed that at night, after all the sheep are fed and happy, he calls each one by name to make sure they are all safe. Then he closes gate to their pen and sleeps at the door to protect them from wolves and thieves. I sure hope he doesn't want me to do that!

"I tell you the truth; I am the gate for the sheep"
John 10:7

I know he gets up with each sunrise and starts to map out the safest path to the next pasture. His job never seems to end!

"He calls his own sheep by name and leads them out"
John 10:3

16

I wonder if that's why he wanted to hire me. He might need someone to stay with those sheep, as he walks the path before them. I don't know if I'm willing to give my life and time for those sheep. Who will keep me safe from those wolves and thieves? I think I'm better off on my own!

"The hired hand will run when he sees a wolf coming.
He will abandon the sheep because they don't
belong to him and he isn't their shepherd"
John 10:12

I do have to admit though; it sure is peaceful out here. Yup, if I were a sheep, I sure would want to be in his flock! Those sheep don't know how lucky they are. That shepherd really does love them. I guess it's pretty nice living under the care of such a good shepherd. Yah, those sheep really do have it made!

"Surely goodness and mercy will follow me all the days of my life."
Psalm 23:6

Ya know, maybe I should give that shepherd a chance after all. It might be real nice getting to know him; someone that caring and loving might even bring a wandering soul like me some peace!

"We are His people and the sheep of His pasture"
Psalm 100:3

Would you?
He's waiting for
your answer!

"I am the good shepherd, I know my sheep and my sheep
know me... I lay down my life for the sheep."
John 10:14-15

Printed in the United States
by Baker & Taylor Publisher Services